Disclaimer:

All rights reserved. No part of this book may be reproduced or transmitted in any form or by any means; electronic, mechanical, photocopying, recording or otherwise without the prior written permission of the publisher. For more information, contact N3D Enterprises.

The ideas expressed in this book are my own and there are no guarantees that you will have success. This book is intended to be for supplemental purposes and is my opinion only. Please consider leaving a review wherever you purchased this book or by informing your friends and family of its availability.

Copyright 2019

All Rights Reserved

Published by N3D Publishing Company

businessownersoftomorrow@gmail.com

https://www.n3denterprises.com

Contact:

Instagram: @businessownersoftomorrow

Facebook: Business Owners of Tomorrow

Teach Kids Business
A Workbook for Kidpreneurs
Nyanna Harris

CONTENTS

#THEBOOT

This workbook offers secrets and tips to make your business a success. You can use it on your own or at one of our workshops. Complete the journal entries and worksheets to help bring your dream business to life. To locate a workshop near you, contact us at bit.ly/teachkidsbiz

This workbook includes:

My Business Idea

Purchasing Inventory

Start-Up Costs

Profit & Loss Statements

Target Audience

Branding & Marketing

Logo

Goal Setting

Business Plan Outline

Enterprising

Your Team

Vocabulary

Vendor Checklist

Explain This to Me

Wikipedia defines entrepreneurship as the process of designing, launching and running a new business, which is often initially a small business. The people who create these businesses are called entrepreneurs.

What fueled your interest in entrepreneurship?

_____
_____
_____
_____
_____
_____
_____

Do you know any other kid entrepreneurs?

_____
_____
_____
_____
_____
_____

Explain This to Me

Kidpreneurs are the same as entrepreneurs. They just happen to be under 18 years of age. We've had the pleasure to meet Kidpreneurs who own all types of businesses from disc jockey, apparel company, bakers, cosmetics and more.

What is one question you would ask a Kidpreneur?

_____

_____

_____

_____

_____

_____

What is one thing you thought was true about being an entrepreneur that you now know is false?

_____

_____

_____

_____

_____

_____

What Is Your BIG Idea?

In the box below, list 3 things you would enjoy doing regardless if you were paid for it or not. Circle the one that is your absolute favorite.

Draw pictures of some possible items you could sell doing what you listed above.

Let's Dig Deeper

In business, entrepreneurs are likely to select things they enjoy as their main business. The goal is to have fun while earning an income.

Do you enjoy doing the three things you listed on the previous page?

_____

_____

_____

_____

_____

_____

Which of those things are you able to do with little to no assistance?

_____

_____

_____

_____

_____

_____

Start-up Costs

Item	Amount

1. What is the total cost of your supplies? _____

2. What is the estimated cost of each item? _____

3. How much should you charge for each product? _____

4. How much profit will you earn? _____

5. How many items can you make with the purchased supplies? _____

Money Talks

Purchasing supplies is a big part of business. As a young adult, you'd likely have to solicit your parent or guardian for the initial investment of funds. Your parents thus become your lenders.

Who else do you know that would invest in your business?

_____
_____
_____
_____
_____
_____
_____

What are you going to do to get them to invest in your business?

_____
_____
_____
_____
_____
_____
_____

Money Talks

Lenders often require a repayment of funds. Do you have a plan to repay your investors?

_____

_____

_____

_____

_____

_____

_____

After you consider the cost of your initial business supplies, how long will it take you to earn a profit?

_____

_____

_____

_____

_____

_____

_____

Sample Profit and Loss Statement

Estimated Sales	Jan.	Feb.	March
Cakes	60	60	30
Cupcakes	150	75	125
Total Sales	210	135	155
Cost of Goods Sold			
Cake Flour	9	9	9
Sugar	6	6	6
Eggs	3	3	3
Butter	9	9	9
Baking Powder	3	3	3
Milk	3	3	3
Flavor	4	4	4
Salt	2	2	2
Total Cost of Goods sold	37	37	37
Gross Profit	**173**	**98**	**118**
Expenses			
Vendor Fees	25	35	40
Business Cards	20	0	0
Website	25	25	25
Total Expenses	70	60	65
Net Income	103	38	53

Profit and Loss Statement

Estimated Sales	Jan.	Feb.	March

Total Sales

Cost of Goods Sold

Total Cost of Goods sold

Gross Profit

Expenses

Total Expenses

Net Income

Competitive Market

You must understand that as an entrepreneur, you are not the only one in that field. There are several different kinds and styles of your business idea in the world.

How will you differentiate yourself?

_____
_____
_____
_____
_____
_____
_____
_____

List below you immediate competitors.

_____
_____
_____
_____
_____
_____

Target Audience: Who are your customers?

Paste customer pictures here.   Describe your customers. (Ages and interest)

Who's Buying That

Acquiring and maintaining customers is a difficult task. With so many avenues available, there is almost no wrong way to locate clients.

What ways will you identify your customers?

_____
_____
_____
_____
_____
_____
_____

Are you prepared to handle a customer who is dissatisfied?

_____
_____
_____
_____
_____
_____
_____

Who's Buying That

Identifying your target audience is key to building a sustainable business. The right or wrong customers will make or break your business.

If you are starting a business educating girls on how to care for their hair, who would be in your target audience?

_____

_____

_____

_____

_____

_____

If your business is selling custom bow ties, who would be in your target audience?

_____

_____

_____

_____

_____

_____

Branding & Marketing

LOGO: Sketch a photo of the picture you want to represent your company.

Branding

Word Scramble

dimea ocisal _____ _____

ormlatfp _____

bsiteew _____

gool _____

ardillbbo _____

dbrna _____

alpernos _____

dienceua _____

larefuc _____

arasetep _____

shgaath _____

Categorize in the order of importance.

___Build your online _____

___Weave your _____ into everything you do

___You are a walking _____

___Be _____ careful what you put on _____ _____

___Business and _____ accounts are _____

___Your _____ , FB, Twitter and IG should have your _____

___Know you _____

___Create your own _____

___Don't aim to please everyone.

Words: billboard, logo, brand, social media, hashtag, careful, platform, website, audience, personal

Social Butterfly

Social Media is very huge at this time. Businesses are literally going from unknown to a million followers from a simple post. It is important to monitor your social media while keeping your business and personal accounts separated.

Will you use social media as a form of advertisement? Why or why not?

_____
_____
_____
_____
_____
_____
_____

Who will monitor your social media accounts?

_____
_____
_____
_____
_____
_____
_____

Social Butterfly

Why is it important to keep your personal and business social media accounts separate?

_____
_____
_____
_____
_____
_____
_____

Identify a scenario where intermingling of social media accounts cost an entrepreneur their business.

_____
_____
_____
_____
_____
_____
_____

Business Owners Of Tomorrow

1. What is advertising?
   _____
   _____
   _____
   _____

2. The following are ways to advertise:
   Flyers, Business Cards, Radio, Word of mouth
   Billboards, TV, Social Media, Parents
   Church, School, Text, Email
   All of the above
   None of the above

3. I do not need a logo. T/F

4. My customers are _____.

5. _____ is the most effective if customers are giving great/positive reviews.

6. Social media can make or break my business. T/F

7. What is a website?
   _____
   _____

8. The cost of advertising is:
   Cheap
   Expensive
   Varies
   None

Kidpreneur Word Search

```
W E O N T M N X T I S G O A L S N O M T N L C O L P N
E N T R E P R E N E U R H I T P O M E N I Y E S U Q W O
A E D I M E T I N T L O P E N A M A R K E T I S P A X J I
L O G O Q I U T I P R O F I T P R O F E T L I N E T M A T
O T S O C Y E S M Y B U S I N E S S O N P L Q O L T R A
S E L L S A L E A N C T V Z M X N E O N B O M M E E N
S S O B W P O L N E O T S T A R T U P L O N E Q O B I O
M A R K E T I N G Q W I P L O M N B C E B S R L S Z B D
L K I W C K I D P R E N E U R I A M B I T I O N M N R E K
G I N S I T R E V D A B I E N T G W S A V E P O D N E P S
B E C O M S U P P L I E S Q V A S P N E V M O O S S P W
```

GOALS	ENTREPRENEUR	LOGO
PROFIT	BUSINESS	SALE
KIDPRENEUR	MARKETING	BOSS
EMPLOYEE	STARTUP	CUSTOMER
LOSS	AMBITION	IDEA
ADVERTISING	DONATION	SAVE
SPEND	SUPPLIES	RESOURCE

Build Your Brand

Branding and marketing will make or break your business. If not done properly, your business will close before it ever even opened. It is absolutely important to spend a great deal of time ensuring you have set up everything appropriately. This is also the area where you will likely spend the most money upfront.

Will you remain committed despite failures, dead ends or other unforeseen circumstances?

_____
_____
_____
_____
_____
_____

How much creative control do you wish to maintain in your business?

_____
_____
_____
_____
_____
_____

Branding & Marketing
How Will You Spread the Word about Your Business?

Partners (family and friends)	Invitations (sponsors, launch event, charity)
Advertisements (flyers, business cards, social media)	Coupons (donations, discount products, testers)

Teamwork Makes the Dream Work

The team you have around you will be critical. Make sure you select people who are responsible, proficient and who really care about your success. You may also consider starting businesses with other people (partnerships or corporations).

Do you feel mentorship in business is necessary?

_____
_____
_____
_____
_____
_____
_____

What other responsibilities will you have in addition to be being a business owner?

_____
_____
_____
_____
_____
_____

Who is on your team?

Job title (Role in your business)	Name (of person assisting)

Save. Spend. Invest.

While running a business, it is important to put money away for the future and donate to charities amongst the spending that will occur.

What is your strategy for saving money?

_____

_____

_____

_____

_____

_____

_____

There are many causes and organizations that you could provide a charitable contribution. List below the organizations that are near and dear to you that could possibly benefit from your business financially.

_____

_____

_____

_____

_____

_____

_____

Business Owners Of Tomorrow

Goal setting

In order to run a successful business, you not only need to know where you are but also where you are going. Setting goals is the best way to determine success as well as keep track of your progress. Below you will find a set of question that will make your goal setting process just a bit easier.

1. How much money do you want to make this year? Month? Week?
2. How much product will you need to sell to meet your goals?
3. How much is your supply total?
4. Do you have the capital necessary to purchase the supplies necessary to meet this goal?
5. What ways can you reach your goal?
6. What is your plan for replication?
7. Do you have an exit strategy? If so, what is it?

Goal Setting Example

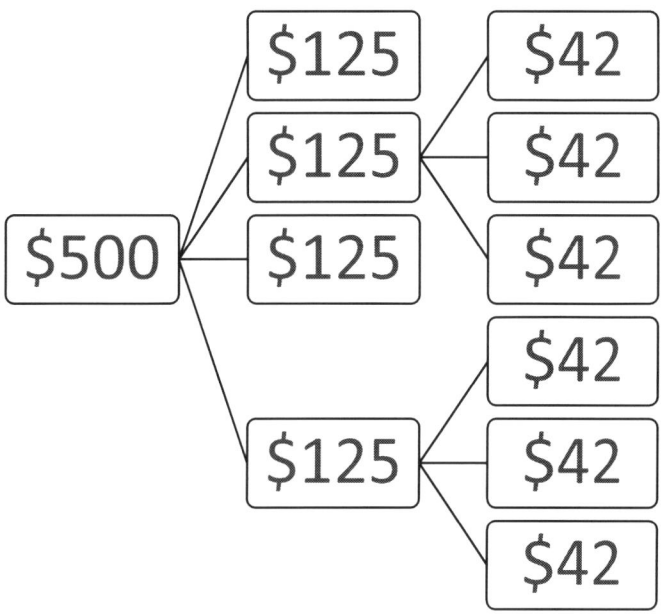

Monthly goal: $500

Weekly goal: $125

Daily goal (3days/week) $42

Example: Cupcakes $2/each = 250 cupcakes OR Cakes $37/each = 14 cakes OR any combination

Destiny can do the following to support reach her goal:

- Promote on social media.
- Contact previous customers.
- Have a sale on black Friday or Small business Saturday
- Ask her friends and family to support her goal.

Goal Setting Template

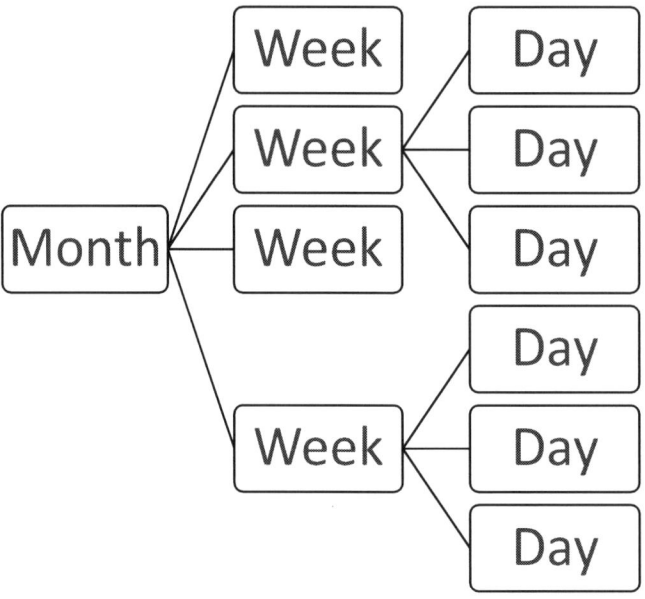

Goal: _____

Weekly goal: _____

Daily Goal: _____

What can you do to reach that goal?

    A. _____
    B. _____
    C. _____
    D. _____

Business Plan Outline

My business name is
_____

My business solves the problem of
_____

The photo that represents my business looks like
_____

Here are some items I will need to get my business started:
_____
_____
_____
_____
_____
_____

My startup costs are estimated at
_____

The audience I am targeting includes
_____

Here are a few of my business goals:
_____
_____

Speak On It

There will be times where you have to speak to people about your products or services. This can be done at a vendor event, a pop-up shop or on stage. Practice answering questions to ensure you are prepared.

Are you comfortable speaking in front of others?

_____

_____

_____

_____

_____

_____

_____

Write out your 30 second elevator pitch.

_____

_____

_____

_____

_____

_____

Winner's Circle

Kids in business do very well and are often awarded for their success. Many have received trophies and cash prizes as well as been invited to television interviews. This is a great way to increase your exposure and solidify your brand.

Are you motivated by awards?

_____
_____
_____
_____
_____
_____

Research and list below Kidpreneurs who have won awards, big or small, for the businesses.

_____
_____
_____
_____
_____
_____

ENTERPRISING

What other ways can your business expand?

Draw pictures of other Big Ideas you may have.

Let's talk expansion

There is one young baker who started her business simply making cupcakes. She has now expanded to include teaching classes for youth and has published her very own cookbook. This is what we call enterprising.

How can you incorporate the products/services listed on the previous plan?

_____

_____

_____

_____

_____

_____

_____

Write out a plan to implement those products/services. Be sure to include a timeline and marketing strategy.

_____

_____

_____

_____

_____

_____

_____

Thinking out Loud

When doing interviews, you will often be asked questions about your future and things you have learned in the process.

What is one piece of advice you would give a future entrepreneur since you've completed this workbook?

_____
_____
_____
_____
_____
_____
_____

List any notes or questions you may have about starting your business here.

_____
_____
_____
_____
_____
_____
_____

Vocabulary

1. Advertising – a fancy word for telling people about your business
2. Boss – the person in charge at your job
3. Business plan – a written description of your business
4. Employee – the worker on a job
5. Entrepreneur – someone who owns his or her own business and works for himself or herself.
6. Ethics – making the right choices for your business
7. Integrity – the quality of being honest and have strong moral principles
8. Labor – the work required to shop for, produce and sell your product
9. Logo – a picture or design that represents your company
10. Needs – things I cannot live without
11. Plagiarism – stealing someone else's idea or information
12. Profit – the amount of money left over after you have purchased your supplies and sold your product
13. Start-up costs – the amount of money you will need to start your business
14. Wants – things I can live without
15. Word of mouth – a way to advertise without spending money. One person tells another and that person tells someone else, etc.

Vendor Display Checklist

THE FOLLOWING ARE ESSENTIAL:

- Table (unless otherwise provided)
- Linen
- Products
- Business Sign
- Pricing Sign/Flyer
- Money Storage Container (Fannie Pack)
- Change for Customers
- Payment Method (Cash, PayPal, Square, Zelle, Cash App)
- Packaging for products (bags, boxes, plates, etc.)

THE FOLLOWING ARE HIGHLY RECOMMENDED:

- Clipboard
- Pen
- Email sign-up sheet
- Business Cards
- Promotional item (raffle, prize, special)

THANK YOU

Business Owners of Tomorrow (#TheBoot) serves as an educational platform that assist youth with creating, launching and successfully running their own businesses. It is a place to learn the fundamentals of entrepreneurship, leadership, public speaking, creative thinking and financial literacy. Most importantly, we serve as a bridge for unique education.

We are seeking you with ambition, desire and confidence who want to help make the world a better place. If that you, then let's get started.

On behalf of #TheBoot, thanks for supporting our Teach Kids Business family. Always remember, Dream Big!

Nyanna Harris, Founder

Made in the USA
Columbia, SC
30 October 2024